GUM GIRL

SHE'S GOT GUM & SHE'S NOT AFRAID TO USE IT!

GUM GIRL

★ ★ IN ★ ★

THE TENTACLES OF DOOM!

ANDI WATSON

WALKER

To my Super-mum and Super-dad

This is a work of fiction. Names, characters, places and incidents
are either the product of the author's imagination or, if real, used fictitiously.

First published 2012 by Walker Books Ltd

87 Vauxhall Walk, London SE11 5HJ

2 4 6 8 10 9 7 5 3 1

Text & Illustrations © 2012 Andi Watson

The right of Andi Watson to be identified as author of this work has been asserted by him
in accordance with the Copyright, Designs and Patents Act 1988

This book has been typeset in Block T

Printed and bound in China

British Library Cataloguing in Publication Data: a catalogue record for this
book is available from the British Library

ISBN 978-1-4063-2940-7

www.walker.co.uk   www.gumgirl.co.uk

GUM GIRL in DIRT & LOATHING

Look at the state of this mess, Grace. I've seen cleaner pigsties.

It's not a mess if I know where everything is.

Where're your favourite jeans?

On the floor.

Your pencil case?

The floor.

Your homework... No, don't answer.

I know there's a carpet under there somewhere and I want to be able to see it.

Tidy up, Grace!

8

9

11

We have a serious situation here.

Potential Code Grey HIVE Infestation.

Sit down, Miss Gibson.

You're at primary school, yet this work looks like advanced chemistry and pharmacology.

You seem very interested in my homework considering you're school health inspectors.

Ha har. Grace loves her science.

Check the lunch box.

Hey, leave my sarnies alone.

Scan results?

Cortisol spike. She's hiding something.

H.Q. I'm raising the alert to a Code Green. Suspicion of infiltration and invasion. Suggest immediate shut down and quarantine in a five-mile radius.

Sh... Shut down? But you haven't seen the school yet.

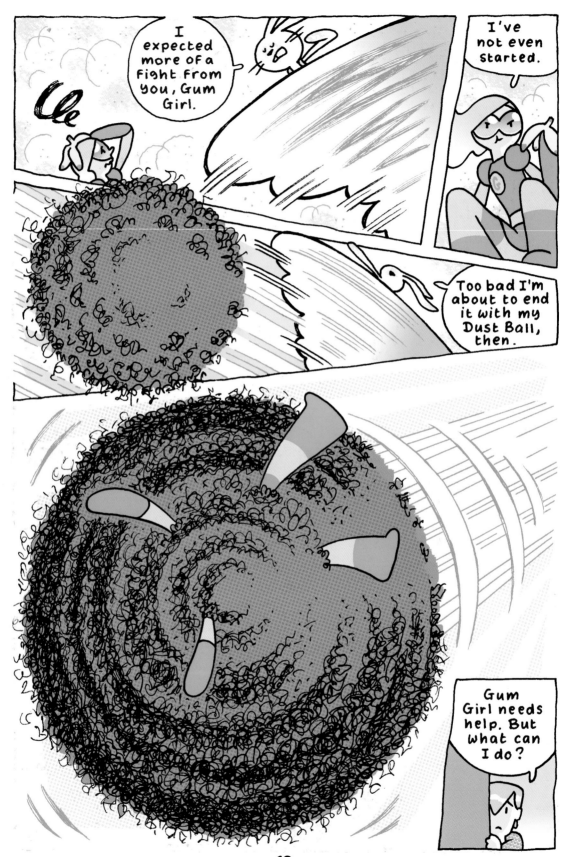

To celebrate passing the health inspection...

...I've decided that we all deserve a special treat.

GUM GIRL in 8-ARMED BANDIT

Please let there be no more homework.

Ever.

So I have organized the first school trip in twenty years.

Oh, great. We'll probably be dragged around an old ruin or something boring.

Who cares? I'm sick of seeing nothing but high-security fences and razor wire.

As the last trip to Mt Misfortune resulted in a helicopter rescue from an active volcano...

My dad still has the scars from that.

Um, nice.

...we'll be going to Catastrophe Aquarium.

Oh, I wanted to get some scars of my own.

I can't wait to see Kevin the Octopus. He's really clever.

I expect everyone to be on their best behaviour. I don't want to have to call any of the emergency services.

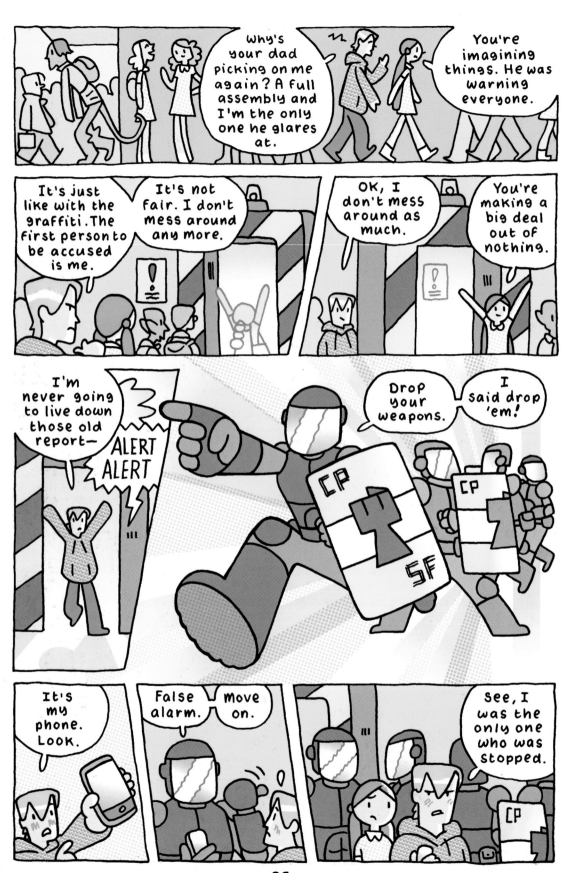

28

What's three thousand, three hundred and sixty-two times twelve?

Kevin is an extremely clever octopus who loves maths. Who would like to ask him a maths question?

My goodness, that's a tough one. Kevin will try and answer the question using the number balls.

I had to use a calculator, but he's right. Forty thousand, three hundred and forty-four.

Will he do my homework?

Sorry, no, but there is something he likes to do for fun.

Juggling.

WOW!

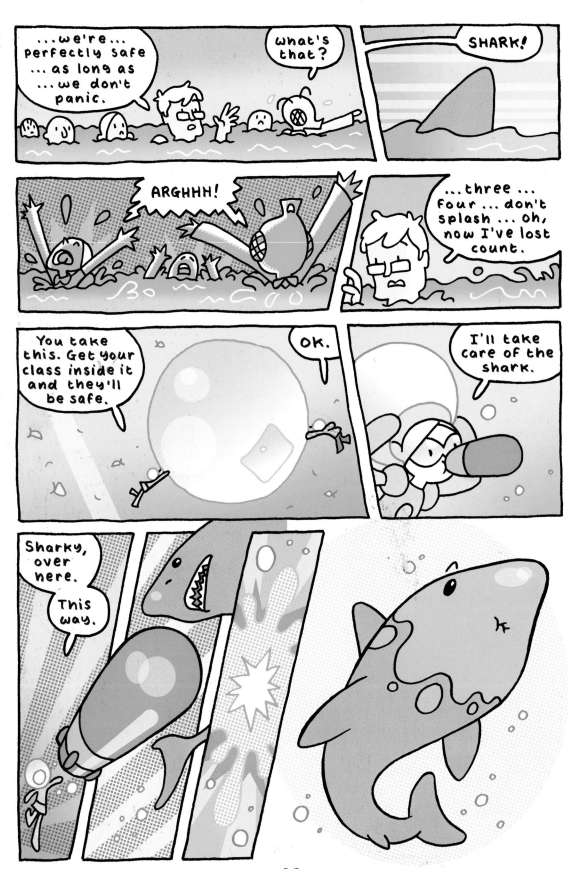

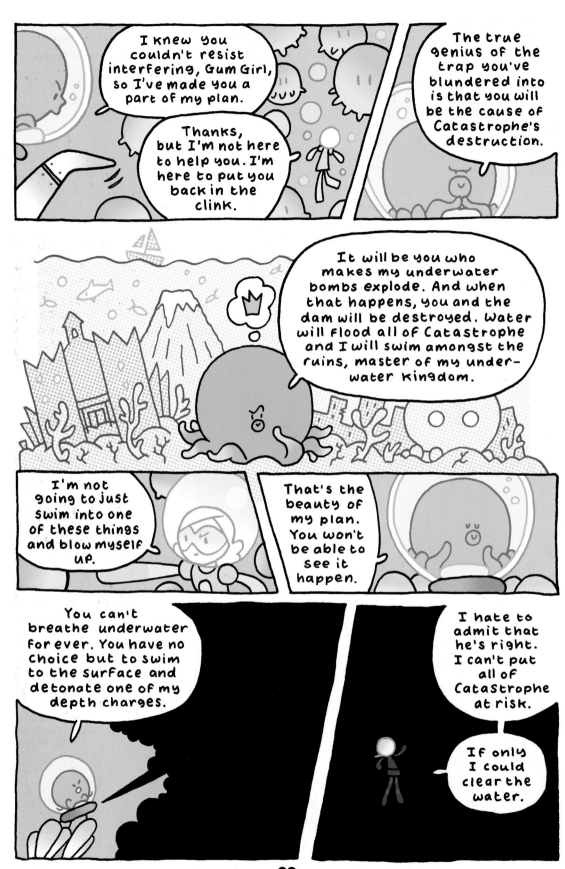

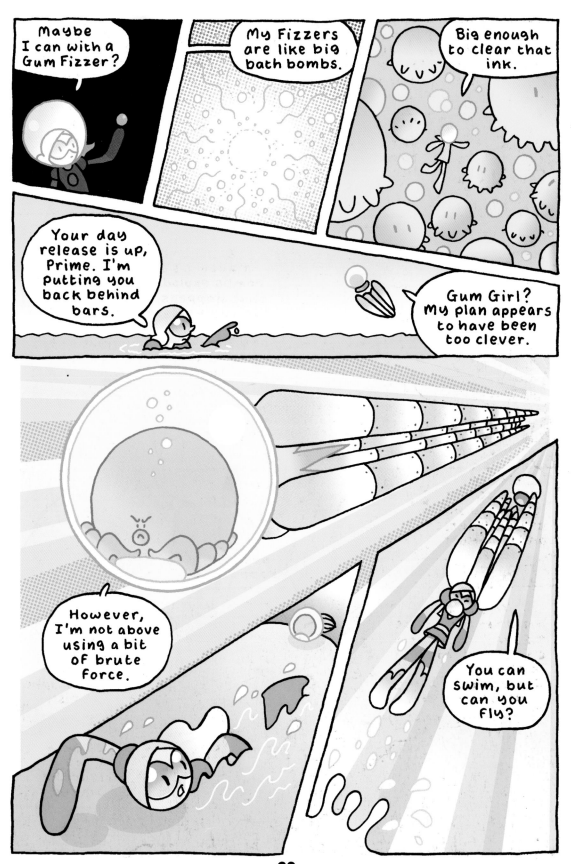

40

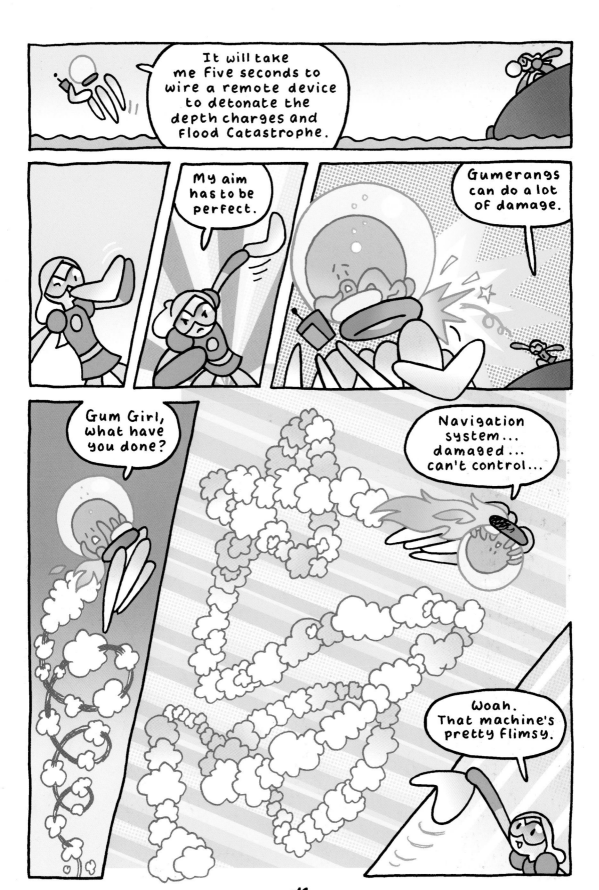

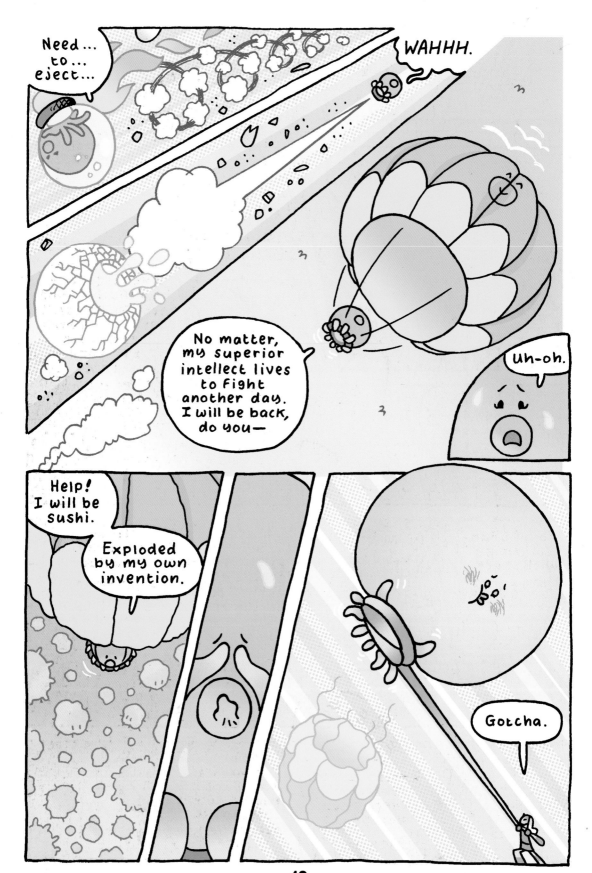

51

55